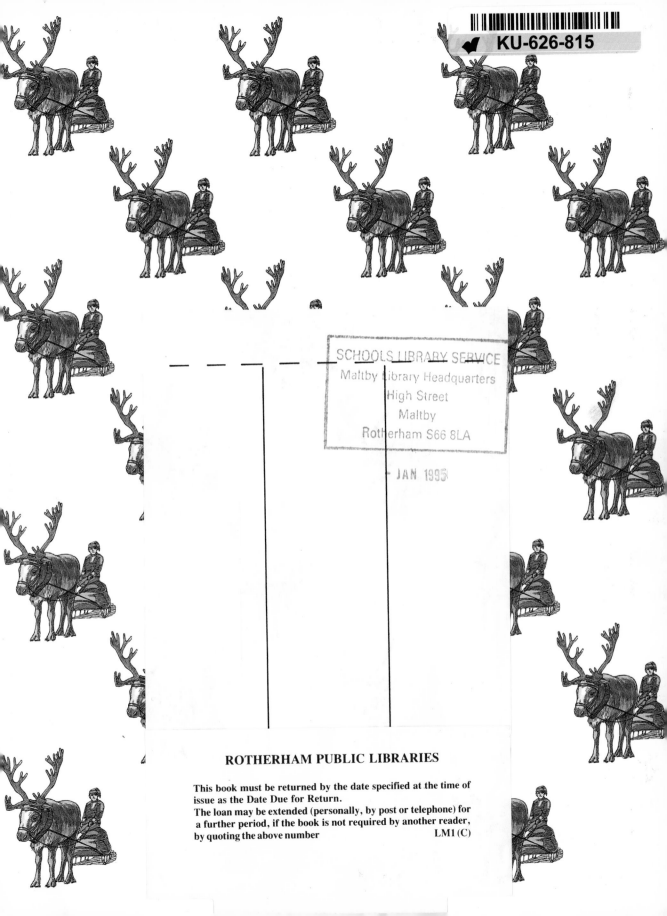

ROTHERHAM PUBLIC LIBRARIES

HOW TO SURVIVE

at the

NORTH POLE

Written by
Anita Ganeri
Illustrated by
Rob Shone

SIMON & SCHUSTER
YOUNG BOOKS

About the author: **Anita Ganeri** has written and edited over 50 books for children, mainly on natural history and the natural world. She has travelled widely and has just returned from a trip to the jungles of Madagascar. She has never been to the North Pole but would quite like to go.

About the consultant: **Antony Mason** is a travel writer and author of books for children on geography and exploration. He is currently working on biographies of Peary and Amundsen.

About the survival expert: **Rob Ferguson** has over 20 years experience of rock climbing and mountaineering in Britain, Europe and Greenland. Many of the expeditions he has been a part of have been in Greenland. The most recent was the 1993 British Lemon Mountain Expedition in East Greenland.

Throughout this book, the name "Inuit" is used to describe the 75,000 or so native Arctic people who used to be known as Eskimos. In their own language, "Inuit" means "the People".

Copyright © S•W Books 1994

Designed and conceived by
S•W Books
28 Percy Street
London W1P 9FF

First published in Great Britain in 1994 by
Simon & Schuster Young Books
Campus 400
Maylands Avenue
Hemel Hempstead
Herts HP2 7EZ

Printed and bound in Belgium by
PROOST International Book Production

British Library Cataloguing in Publication Data available

ISBN 0 7500 1552 7
ISBN 0 7501 0782 0 (pb)

CONTENTS

INTRODUCTION

If it's sun, sea and sandy beaches you're after, the North Pole may not be the place for you! It is icy cold, windy and a very long way from home. But, if your holiday plans backfired and you suddenly found yourself stranded at the North Pole, how would you survive? Could you harness a husky, construct an igloo or spear a seal for supper? More to the point, would you know how to keep warm even in temperatures well below freezing? Don't worry! With this book and a local Inuit to guide you, you'll soon be a hardy polar explorer. And although the North Pole is your base, you'll be able to read about life at the South Pole too.

WARNING! ONLY TRY THE SURVIVAL TIPS IN THIS BOOK WITH YOUR INUIT GUIDE'S APPROVAL.

What comes to mind when you think of the North Pole? Ice, ice and more ice? It really does feel as if you are at the end of the Earth. But there is more to the North Pole than meets the eye. For a start, there are amazing animals, including seals, whales and polar bears. In fact, the word 'Arctic' comes from an ancient Greek word for bear.

FROZEN LANDSCAPE

The scenery at both the North and South Poles is constantly changing as the ice moves and creates new features. If you hear a strange creaking sound on your travels, don't panic. It's not a wild ice beast out to get you but the ice itself cracking up and crashing together. A mixture of icescape features are shown on the right. Make sure you know which ones to avoid.

Permanent pack ice
Ice forms at the ocean edges in winter and melts in summer. But some pack ice remains all year round.

Crevasses
Crevasses are huge cracks in glaciers up to 40 m deep and ready to swallow up careless explorers.

THE ARCTIC

The ice at the North Pole is frozen ocean - there isn't any land. But the North Pole is part of a larger area - the Arctic. It includes Greenland, covered in a thick ice sheet, Spitsbergen and a band of land, called the tundra, in the northern parts of Canada, Alaska, Russia and Scandinavia.

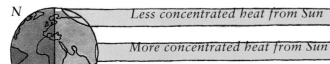

Less concentrated heat from Sun

More concentrated heat from Sun

SURVIVAL TIP 1

In summer, the ice at the ocean edges begins to melt. A perfectly safe looking piece of ice can suddenly crack and shift. Keep clear! Your chances of survival in the icy water are small.

Glacier
A glacier is a river of ice which flows very, very slowly into the sea from icecaps and mountains. The Greenland coast is streaked with glaciers.

COLDER AT THE POLES

The Poles are the coldest places on Earth. This is because the Earth has a curved surface and the Sun's rays hit the Poles at a wide angle so they are weak and spread out. They hit the Equator full on so it is very hot.

Ice floe
An ice floe is a large sheet of floating ice. Polar bears use passing ice floes as rafts.

Icebergs
Icebergs are huge chunks of ice which break off glaciers and ice shelves. Only a tenth of an iceberg shows above the water. Ships beware!

Ice shelf
An ice shelf is a flat area of permanent ice floating on the sea. It forms when a glacier flows and floats into the sea.

SPOT THE POLE

After a while, ice all starts to look the same. To work out which Pole you're at, look for animal clues. There are no penguins at the North Pole. Polar bears, but no penguins!

THE ANTARCTIC

The South Pole stands in the middle of the ice-capped continent of Antarctica. The icecap contains 90 per cent of all the ice on Earth. It is 3 km thick in places and so heavy the land has bowed under its weight.

WHERE IN THE WORLD?

Nothing at the North and South Poles marks the spot, but they are fixed points at either end of the Earth's axis. These are the geographical poles. They are not the same as the magnetic poles which are always changing. At the moment, the magnetic North Pole is somewhere in Canada. The polar regions are said to be the areas inside the Arctic and Antarctic Circles, at latitudes 66°N 32°S .

THE NORTH POLE

The North Pole sits in the middle of the frozen Arctic Ocean. Parts of the ocean and surrounding land are permanently covered in ice but the ice doubles in quantity in the winter months.

PEOPLES OF THE NORTH

People have lived in the Arctic for thousands of years. They include the Inuit, the Lapps of Scandinavia and the Evenk and Chukchi of Siberia.

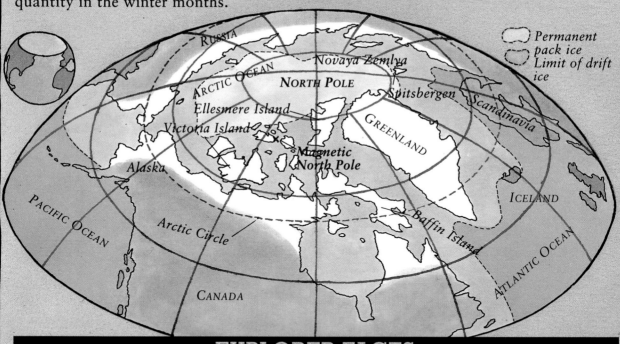

RUSSIA
ARCTIC OCEAN
Novaya Zemlya
NORTH POLE
Spitsbergen
Scandinavia
Ellesmere Island
Victoria Island
GREENLAND
Magnetic North Pole
Alaska
ICELAND
PACIFIC OCEAN
Arctic Circle
Baffin Island
ATLANTIC OCEAN
CANADA

Permanent pack ice
Limit of drift ice

EXPLORER FACTS

The American, Robert Peary, claimed to have reached the North Pole on 6 April 1909. Many experts don't believe him. Some reports (also doubtful) say that Frederick Cook got there a year earlier.

THE OZONE HOLE

The ozone layer protects us from the Sun's harmful UV rays. But scientists have found a hole in the ozone layer above Antarctica, caused by man-made CFC gases.

HUMAN PRESENCE

There are no native people at the South Pole - it's far too cold. But hundreds of scientists work on research bases and thousands of tourists visit by ship and plane. And, of course, there's the odd explorer!

THE SOUTH POLE

The South Pole is located on a plateau of ice 2,606 km from the edge of the Antarctic Circle, and 2,835 m above sea level. The ice sheet covering Antarctica is one and a half times the size of the USA.

US Amundsen-Scott Station

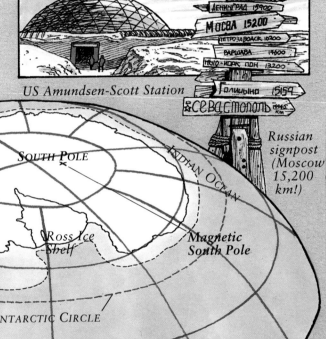

Russian signpost (Moscow 15,200 km!)

ATLANTIC OCEAN

SOUTH POLE

INDIAN OCEAN

Filchner Ice Shelf

Palmer Land

Ross Ice Shelf

Magnetic South Pole

SOUTH AMERICA

ANTARCTIC CIRCLE

PACIFIC OCEAN

EXPLORER FACTS

Roald Amundsen (1872-1928)

The first person to reach the South Pole, on 14 December 1911, was the Norwegian explorer, Roald Amundsen. He used Inuit-style clothes and supplies and husky-drawn sledges.

SHELTERING FROM THE ENVIRONMENT

Your worst enemies at the North Pole are the freezing cold and biting wind. You need warm clothes and shelter to keep frostbite and hypothermia at bay. The local Arctic people are very hardy and have learnt to cope with the conditions. And although their lives are being changed by contact with the outside world, they still know about survival. So take a leaf out of your Inuit guide's book.

WEARING THE RIGHT GEAR

The golden rule for keeping warm is to wear several thin layers of clothes, not just one thick layer. The layers trap air between them for insulation. However, your clothes should not be too hot or heavy. If you get too warm, you'll sweat and this will draw heat away from your body. Inuit clothes are made from animal skin but there are also very warm, man-made fabrics to choose from.

Undergear

Woollen jumper or shirt

Thick trousers

Thermal underwear

Wool socks

The glare from the Sun and snow is bright enough to blind you. Always wear sunglasses or goggles.

A windproof, waterproof, insulating jacket is a must. It should be thick but not too cumbersome.

Snowshoes are good for walking over soft snow. Skis are better on harder ice and snow.

Waterproof container for holding essentials such as sun cream, lip salve and matches.

Keep your hands warm inside mittens. Bare fingers might get frostbitten.

Padded, insulating trousers help keep the heat in. Tuck them firmly into your boots.

Wear several pairs of wool socks, with sturdy, waterproof boots.

THE INUIT

The local Inuit people have many physical features and adaptations to help them survive in the Arctic cold. Their heavy eyelids help protect their eyes from glare. They are short and solidly built to help their bodies conserve heat. They have thick pads of fat on their cheeks and eyelids, to protect these parts which are exposed to the cold.

The sealskin outer tunic is worn fur side out. The hood is trimmed with wolverine fur, the only fur on which moisture from the breath does not freeze solid.

The Inuit wear large, fur mittens. They also pull their hands inside their tunic sleeves for warmth.

Trousers are made of reindeer or polar bear skin. They are tucked into the boots.

An Inuit wears sealskin 'socks', fur side in and lined with warm, soft moss. He also wears several pairs of boots, one on top of the other.

SURVIVAL TIP 2

The glare of the Sun reflected off the ice can cause temporary snow blindness. Always wear sunglasses or goggles to protect your eyes. Make your own goggles from bark, cloth or cardboard with small slits cut in. The Inuit carve goggles out of ivory or wood.

Inner clothing
The inner tunic, trousers and socks have the fur on the inside.

Tunic

Trousers

Over-boots

THE ICE AGES

The Earth goes through cycles of bitterly cold, then warmer weather. In the last Ice Age, ice covered about a third of the Earth and woolly mammoths roamed just south of its edge. It ended about 10,000 years ago. Some of the ice covering Greenland and Antarctica is millions of years old.

	WIND SPEED (MPH)			
TEMPERATURE (°C)	10	20	30	40
0	-1	-7	-12	-12
5	-9	-15	-18	-21
0	-12	-18	-23	-26
-5	-18	-26	-32	-35
-10	-26	-34	-40	-43
-15	-31	-42	-48	-51
-20	-40	-51	-57	-60
-25	-43	-54	-62	-65
-30	-51	-62	-70	-74
-35				

The wind chill factor
The stronger the wind, the colder it feels. If the wind was blowing at 48 km/h and the temperature was -34° C, you would freeze solid in just 30 seconds!

THE CLIMATE

The Poles are the coldest and windiest places on Earth. The North Pole has a long, dark winter with temperatures as low as -50° C and gale-force winds. Its summer temperatures are over 10° C. At the South Pole, the temperature plummets below -70° C in winter and never gets above freezing even in summer.

Snow white
Many Arctic animals like the snowy owl have white fur or feathers for camouflage. Foxes and hares are brown in summer but turn white in winter.

LAND OF THE MIDNIGHT SUN

In summer, the North Pole has 24-hour daylight. In winter, it is dark for weeks. This is because the Arctic is tilted towards or away from the Sun. The seasons are reversed at the South Pole as it is in the southern hemisphere.

No Sun

Midnight Sun

Sun

ADAPTING TO THE CLIMATE

Arctic animals and plants have to adapt to the harsh conditions, too. Plants grow very slowly and close to the ground to save energy and keep out of the wind. Animals have survival features such as thick fur coats. Some animals migrate or hibernate in winter.

Polar bears
Polar bears have broad, hairy feet for gripping the ice. They have oily, waterproof fur and compact bodies to cut down heat loss.

Captain Robert Scott's attempt to be the first at the South Pole was foiled by Amundsen who beat him to it by 25 days. Scott reached the South Pole on 18 January 1912 only to find the Norwegian flag and bitter disappointment waiting for him. He and his party died on their way back, from frostbite and starvation.

Scott's grave

Seals
Seals and whales have a thick layer of insulating fat, or blubber, under their skins. Seal blubber may be 10 cm thick.

SURVIVAL TIP 3

If, on your travels, the sky begins to glow with eerie red and green lights - don't panic! These are the famous Northern Lights, or aurora borealis. They are caused by electrical particles from the Sun colliding with gases in the atmosphere.

Small mammals
In winter, some small Arctic mammals hibernate. Others, such as lemmings, stay awake but keep warm and snug under the snow.

Plants
Lichens grow very slowly to save energy. A patch the size of a postage stamp may have taken 100 years to grow.

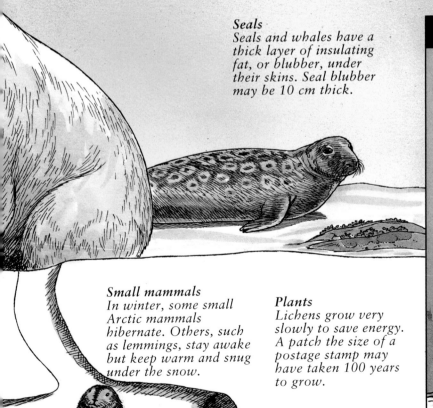

SHELTER FROM THE COLD

Today, many Arctic people live in small, modern houses in towns. On these pages, however, you can find out about their traditional homes and shelters which used local building materials, such as ice. The ice igloo is the most famous type of Inuit shelter. But it is only a temporary shelter, still used on hunting trips. In summer, the Inuit lived in skin tents and, in winter, in houses made of stone and turf. This is because the Inuit traditionally lived as nomadic hunters, with different homes for different seasons.

In winter, the Inuit lived in small houses made of stone with turf packed into any cracks. They were lit by lamps burning seal blubber.

Skin tent

Igloo entrance
The entrance tunnel is sunk lower than the floor of the igloo. This stops cold air getting inside and keeps the igloo surprisingly warm.

Smooth walls
The inner walls are covered in snow which melts, then freezes into a smooth covering of ice.

CHUKCHI TENTS

The Chukchi are Siberian reindeer hunters. They lead nomadic lives, following their herds. They live in reindeer skin tents which are tightly sealed to keep precious warmth in.

BUILDING AN IGLOO

Working from inside, lay a circle of snow blocks (1) and build up more blocks into a spiral (2).

Fit the key block on top (3), fill any cracks with snow and carefully tunnel your way out (4).

SURVIVAL TIP 4

You've watched the experts and now it's your turn to find a cosy place to sleep! You could either tunnel into a snowdrift and build a snowhole, or dig a pit under a tree. Don't forget to leave an air hole for ventilation. **Don't ever try this without expert help!**

Air hole

Tunnel

Raised platform

Snowhole

Treepit shelter

Raised platform
Inside the igloo, people sleep on a large platform, raised off the cold floor and covered with furs and pelts. Blubber lamps and their own body heat keep them snug and warm, no matter how icy the blizzards raging outside.

Permafrost melts

Cold air

HOMES ON THE PERMAFROST

The top of the tundra thaws in summer but the permafrost below stays frozen. But warm homes melt the permafrost and sink into it. They have to be built so cold air can flow underneath.

EATING WITHOUT BEING EATEN

You'll need plenty to eat at the North Pole. Just keeping warm uses up lots of calories (as does running away from polar bears). For such a cold place, there is a huge variety of plants and animals in the Arctic. Local people know exactly which ones to hunt, fish and herd for food. They have no problem storing food for winter. After all, they live in the biggest deep freeze on Earth!

HUNTING

The Inuit are skilled hunters. Seals are a vital part of their diet and they have various methods of catching them. Using the utok method, a hunter crawls up to a seal basking on the ice. He pretends to be just another seal until he is close enough to harpoon his prey.

Many Inuit now have modern hunting weapons such as rifles. They crawl towards the seals, well hidden behind a white screen, then shoot. The rifle is fired through a hole in the middle of the screen so the hunter stays hidden.

THE MAUPOK METHOD

The maupok or waiting method of hunting is used in winter when the seals spend most of their time in the sea under the ice. The hunter waits patiently by a seal's breathing hole until it comes up for air. Then he plunges his harpoon in. *(right)*

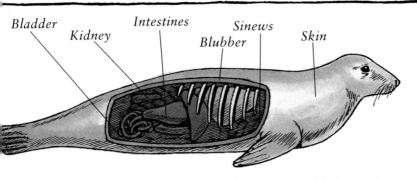

Bladder — Kidney — Intestines — Sinews — Blubber — Skin

SURVIVAL TIP 5

Steer clear of polar bear liver, however peckish you are. It contains a lethal amount of vitamin A. Bear steaks should always be well cooked, to avoid disease.

USING ALL THE BITS

Every bit of a seal is used - nothing is wasted. The skin is used for clothes and tents; the blubber for fuel; the sinews for sewing and the bones for tools. Bladders are made into windows for winter houses. The meat and innards are eaten, raw or cooked. Dried seal intestines are a particular delicacy!

Walrus — Polar bear — Seal — Narwhal — Caribou

Greenland whale

THE HARPOON

The seal harpoon has a detachable pointed head, connected to a line. The point sticks in the seal and pulls loose. Then the hunter draws the seal in.

HUNTER'S QUARRY

If an Inuit invites you to supper, expect to find some of the animals above on the menu. Leave the hunting to the experts - walruses can turn nasty!

Seal harpoon

FISHING

The sea under the ice and along the coasts of the Arctic Ocean teems with fish, and these play a very important part in the Inuit diet. As with hunting, the Inuit use a mixture of traditional and modern methods to catch them. Salmon and Arctic char are caught as they migrate up river in the summer. Semi-circular stone weirs are set up to guide the fish into range and trap them, then the Inuit stab them with special fish spears, called leisters. In winter, model fish are jiggled in holes in the ice, to tempt the real fish to the surface. Left-over fish is dried and smoked, then stored for winter.

Leister

Drying fish

REINDEER HERDING

The Lapps of northern Scandinavia and the Chukchi of Siberia are reindeer herders. They live nomadic lives, following the reindeer as they graze on lichens and grasses. They eat reindeer

Lapps herding reindeer across a river

meat, milk and cheese and use reindeer skins for making tents and clothes and for trading for other goods. The whole family follows the herd, its belongings strapped on to the reindeer themselves or carried on reindeer-drawn sledges. The herders travel on skis. It's not easy keeping the herd together. The reindeer have to be constantly rounded up.

Lapp mother and child

EXPLORER FACTS

The anthropologist Vilhjalmur Stefanson (1879-1962) lived among the Inuit for many years. He learned to live off the Arctic, without outside supplies.

Stone weir

SURVIVAL TIP 6

If you fancy fish for lunch, try your hand at Arctic-style fishing. Break some holes in the ice. Set up a hook and line in each, marked by a flag. When a fish takes the bait, the flag jerks upright. Pull the fish in quickly - before a seal beats you to it.

HARVESTING PLANTS

The North Pole might not seem the ideal place for plants to grow but, as usual, it's full of surprises. In the short summer months, the tundra bursts into colourful bloom and there are bilberries, cranberries and crowberries galore. You can also find masses of moss and lichen, just ripe for the picking. One of the most nutritious Arctic plants is the Arctic willow. Its shoots and leaves contain more vitamin C than an orange. And how about blubber with crowberry sauce for a nourishing snack!

Arctic willow

Bilberry

Cranberry

Crowberry

Lichens Iceland moss, reindeer moss and rock tripe are all edible lichens. Lichen fermented in a caribou's stomach is a favourite Inuit dish!

EXPLORER FACTS

Willem Barents (1550-1597) had the dubious honour of becoming the first European to spend winter in the Arctic when he was stranded searching for the North East Passage. His crew built a homely hut out of driftwood and ships' timbers and waited for the thaw.

Bird catching *Bolas are used to catch birds. The hunter swings his bola round his head like a lasso, then lets it fly into the flock.*

Bird bola

DELICACIES

To make kiviak, an extra-special Inuit delicacy, stuff 80 little auks into a sealskin. Bury the skin under some rocks for six months until the birds are ready to eat! Another speciality is narwhal skin, hung outside for several months to give it a nutty, chewy taste.

A YEAR'S EATING

WINTER
Fresh seal meat
Dried walrus
Smoked fish
Arctic fox
Polar bear (occasionally!)

SUMMER
Fresh fish (salmon, char)
Canada goose
Little auk
Guillemot eggs
Berries
Whale (occasionally!)
Caribou

SUMMER CAMP

The Inuit's summer camp is a hive of activity as birds, fish and caribou are caught and plants gathered to build up reserves of food for winter. In many camps today, modern cotton and nylon tents have replaced traditional skin tents but the summer camp is still a vital part of the Inuit's year.

THE INUIT DIET

The Inuit's diet is designed to keep them warm. It is also very healthy. The Inuit rarely suffer from heart disease or cancer because their diet is rich in animal proteins and fish. And they have good teeth because they don't eat sweets!

ANIMALS OF THE ARCTIC

When you're as experienced as an Inuit at Arctic survival, you'll know at once which animals to avoid. Until then, here's a mini-guide to some of the creatures you might come across, dangerous and otherwise. A couple of tips - don't mess with polar bears, they are the largest carnivores on land. And keep well away from a walrus's tusks! Most Arctic animals live in the ocean itself and on the tundra. The best time to see them is in summer, when there are plenty of plants on the tundra and algae in the sea for them to eat.

Kittiwake

Little auk

Snowy owl

Musk ox

Polar bear

Caribou (reindeer)

Razorbill

Arctic fox

Eider duck

Narwhal

Bearded seal

Guillemot

Arctic cod

Ringed seal

Walrus

Harp seal

Arctic char

Bowhead whale

20

ANIMALS OF THE ANTARCTIC

Nothing much lives on the frozen wastes of Antarctica but the sea around the continent teems with life. Thousands of seals, whales and penguins feed on tiny, shrimp-like creatures, called krill, which live in their millions in the sea. They, in turn, feed on blooms of algae which live on the underneath of the ice. Antarctic animals have many techniques for survival. Penguins have waterproof feathers and a thick layer of blubber under their skin. Some fish have anti-freeze in their blood to stop their bodies freezing in the icy water.

Right whale

Skua

Elephant seal

Snow petrel

Fur seal

Albatross

Leopard seal

Adelie penguin

Chinstrap penguin

Cormorant

Emperor penguin

Rockhopper penguin

Ross seal

Gentou penguin

Crabeater seal

Orca (Killer whale)

King penguin

Weddell seal

Blue whale

GETTING ON WITH THE LOCALS

Local Arctic people have their own beliefs, customs and culture. Your chances of survival will be greatly improved if you respect their way of life. Inuit society is usually friendly, even to strange explorers as long as they behave themselves! Each family keeps open house. Special occasions are celebrated by feasting, singing, dancing and storytelling. Here's what you might expect on an evening out.

THE STORY OF SEDNA

The Inuit's beliefs are closely linked to nature. Sedna is the all-important sea goddess. Legend says that Sedna was kidnapped by a bird-spirit disguised as a handsome stranger. Her father rescued her, much to the bird-spirit's anger. He caused a terrible storm to hit their boat. To calm the gods, Sedna's father threw her overboard. As she clung to the boat, he chopped off her fingers. These became the seals, walruses and whales.

TUPILAK MAGIC

Tupilaks are Inuit spirits which take the form of ugly monsters. The Inuit carve tupilak figures out of ivory or stone, then tell the spirits to perform tasks such as killing an enemy. A selection of Tupilaks are shown below.

22

EXPLORER FACTS

The first Viking settlers arrived in Greenland in AD982, led by Erik the Red. He had already been banished from Norway and Iceland for murder. The Vikings eventually left Greenland 500 years later.

THE GOOSE AND THE RAVEN

The Inuit love to listen to stories told by the angakok (magician). Are you sitting comfortably? Then I'll begin...

Long ago, when the birds were getting their colours, the goose and the raven agreed to paint each other's feathers. The raven painted the goose black and white. But the goose simply splashed the raven all over with black paint, and that is why ravens are black.

A DRUM AND A DANCE

The Inuit have an unusual way of settling their differences. They play the drums! The opponents face each other, stripped to the waist, and sing and beat their tambourine-like drums. Whoever sings the loudest, or comes up with the most insults, is the winner. You can also wrestle an opponent with your little finger!

CARVINGS

Carving is an ancient Inuit art. Many of the carvings are of the animals that the Inuit people depend upon for survival, such as whales or polar bears. Some are worn as amulets or good luck charms to bring the wearer success in hunting. Others symbolise animal spirits. The Inuit use local materials for their carvings - walrus ivory, whale or seal bone, reindeer antler and soapstone. The ivory pipe above is decorated with scenes from a whale hunt. The details are scratched in the ivory, then filled with soot. This technique is called scrimshaw. The carvings on the chain below represent some of the most important things in an Inuit's life - a sledge, a kayak, a seal, a walrus and a polar bear.

Chain of life

TATTOOING

It used to be traditional for Inuit girls to have their faces tattooed to make them look more beautiful. Luckily for girls today, tattoos have gone out of fashion.

Traditional bow-drill

TOOLS OLD AND NEW

Traditionally, Inuit craftsmen used ivory bow-drills (above) for carving. Today, they use modern tools such as files and vices. Inuit carvings are now made for sale all over the world.

Drum handle

Whale spirit

Polar bear

Carved ivory pipe

MAKING CLOTHES

While the men go out hunting, the women have the all-important job of making clothes. First, they prepare the skins (below), then cut them into shape with their knives and sew them together with bone needles and sinew thread. As a finishing touch, the clothes may be decorated with beadwork or embroidery.

Beadwork

1. The blubber and fat are scraped off.

2. The skin is stretched.

3. The skin is chewed to soften it.

THE CHILDREN'S WORLD

Inuit children have to learn survival and hunting skills at an early age. But it's not all work and no play. They also have toys such as sealskin balls and whips, toy sledges and fish spears, and dolls carved from ivory. Two favourite games are ajagaq and nuglutang. The aim of ajagaq is to jerk a piece of bone on to a pointer. The aim of nuglutang is to spear a swinging piece of ivory. Neither game is as easy as it looks - to play or say!

Ball and whip

The game of Nuglutang

The game of Ajagaq

It's time to find your way back from the North Pole, and it's not going to be easy. It's hard work keeping track of where you are on the vast, fairly featureless expanse of ice. Don't try to fix your position by an iceberg - they tend to drift away! It's far quicker to hitch a lift on a passing Inuit dog sledge or even a skidoo. When you get to the water, you can transfer into a kayak. Remember this - one dog on its own is not enough!

BY SLEDGE

The best way of travelling over the ice, on hunting or trading trips, is by sledge. Inuit sledges are pulled by very hardy Husky dogs. Sledges are made from bone, ivory or wood slats

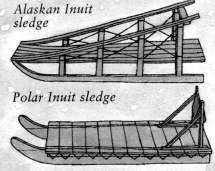

Alaskan Inuit sledge

Polar Inuit sledge

East Greenland sledge

tied together with sealskin thongs between two long runners. To make them glide more smoothly, the runners are covered in soft mud which is left to freeze solid. It is then coated with water which freezes into a small ice surface.

Types of sledge
There are many different types of sledge, for different conditions. Some have narrow runners for hard ice; others wide runners for soft snow.

HARNESSING DOG POWER

Dogs are harnessed in different ways to suit the conditions. The fan hitch (top) is best for open country. The feather hitch (bottom) is good in wooded areas where more control in needed.

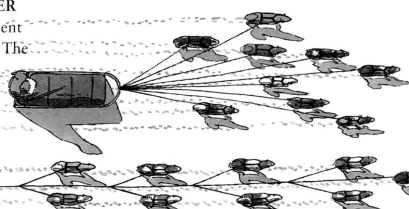

A DOG'S LIFE

Huskies are extremely strong, hardy dogs. A team of 12 can pull a fully loaded sledge weighing half a tonne. Thanks to their thick coats, huskies can survive quite happily in temperatures as low as -45° C - perfect for the Arctic.

In 1897, Salomon Andree of Sweden tried to fly to the North Pole in a hot-air balloon. Just three days after take-off, the balloon was brought down by ice and fog. The crew survived for two months on a diet of bear meat, but eventually died.

SLEIGH BELLS RINGING

Lapland's most famous and most popular resident, Father Christmas, uses a reindeer sledge to get about in. Unlike most Lapp sledges, however, this one can fly!

BY SKIDOO

Modern forms of Arctic transport include skidoos and snowmobiles. In many places, these have taken the place of traditional dog sledges. The Inuit can now trade for skidoos at large, modern stores.

EXPLORER FACTS

When his ship was crushed by the Antarctic ice in 1914, Ernest Shackleton was forced to row 1,280 km over the world's wildest seas to fetch help. Every member of his crew was saved.

GETTING IN OR OUT

The movement of ice at both Poles makes travel very hazardous indeed. In summer, there is the danger of the ice melting and breaking up without warning. In winter, there is the problem of the ice closing in. Many early polar explorers saw their ships smashed to pieces by the ice. Today, huge ships called icebreakers are used to keep trade routes clear from ice in the winter.

Icebreaker

Traditional kayak

THE KAYAK

Kayaks are traditional Inuit boats. They are light and narrow for paddling down rivers in search of caribou, or at sea in search of seals and walruses. They are made of wood or bone, covered in sealskin.

BOATING AND WHALING

In spring and summer, boats really come into their own in the Arctic. Large skin umiaks are used for carrying people and cargo, and for hunting whales. In Alaska, eight-man crews set out each spring to hunt bowhead whales. They are only allowed six harpoon hits a year, so it pays to be accurate. Umiaks are traditionally rowed along but some are now fitted with outboard motors.

Aircraft and helicopters are being used more and more to ferry scientists, oil workers and tourists to the Poles. They also bring in supplies of food, fuel and so on to Inuit settlements in the Arctic. If you're in a hurry, flag one down!

SURVIVAL TIP 8

 1. Compasses aren't very reliable at the North Pole because they point south towards the magnetic North Pole.

2. Never travel alone. If you lose your way or break a leg there'll be no one to help you.

3. Don't touch cold metal with your bare hands. They will stick to it.

 4. Drink at least a litre of water a day to prevent dehydration.

5. Never camp on sea ice. It can break up in a matter of minutes and you'll find yourself floating off out to sea.

6. Avoid alcohol, except in very small quantities. You could die if you don't have your wits about you.

POLES IN PERIL

The first explorers reached the North and South Poles less than 100 years ago. Since then, many things have changed. Outside influences are changing the traditional Arctic way of life. And the Poles themselves are at risk of being destroyed as their rich oil and mineral resources are exploited. The danger is that the fragile polar environment might not be able to stand the onslaught.

THE GOOD, THE BAD AND THE UGLY

The good news is that scientists working at the Poles are making valuable discoveries about the weather and wildlife, such as the hidden world of fish, corals and anemones underneath the ice. And conservation groups are pressing to have Antarctica declared a World Park to protect it. On the down side, however, some countries are still hunting large numbers of endangered species of whales, despite a worldwide ban on commercial whaling. Pollution has become a major problem at the Poles. Junk and rubbish dumps litter the ice. There is the risk of oil spills from tankers. And the ugly oil rigs themselves are hazards to ships.

Whaling continues despite a worldwide ban.

GLOSSARY

Anthropologist A scientist who studies the peoples of the world.

Axis The imaginary line running through the Earth, from top to bottom.

Blubber A layer of thick fat under a seal, whale or penguin's skin.

Caribou Another name for a reindeer.

CFC Short for chlorofluorocarbon, a man-made gas found in aerosol sprays, fridges and foam packaging.

Frostbite A condition caused by bitter cold. Frostbitten fingers and toes may have to be amputated.

Hibernate To go into a deep sleep, to avoid the worst of the winter cold.

Hypothermia A condition caused by a sharp drop in your body temperature. It can kill you.

Icecap A huge, thick sheet of ice. Icecaps cover much of Greenland and Antarctica.

Insulation The way in which warmth is kept in, for example by wearing layers of clothes which trap the air between them.

Lichens Very hardy plants which are a mixture of fungi and algae.

Nomadic Nomadic people wander from place to place in search of food for themselves or their animals. They don't settle in one place for long.

Pack ice The sea ice which forms around the edges of the Arctic Ocean. Some pack ice never melts. But some forms in winter and melts in summer.

Permafrost The permanently frozen soil beneath the topsoil of the tundra.

Snow blindness Partial blindness or dulling of sight caused by the reflection of light on snow.

Tundra The bleak, icy land between the Arctic proper and the northern forests.

Wolverine A fierce Arctic animal which looks like a small bear but is actually part of the weasel family. It feeds on reindeer. It is also called a glutton.

INDEX